New Architecture in New Haven

The MIT Press   Cambridge, Massachusetts, and London, England

New Architecture in New Haven
Revised Edition

Don Metz

Copyright © 1966, 1973 by
The Massachusetts Institute of Technology

All rights reserved. No part of this book may be reproduced in any form or by any means, electronic or mechanical, including photocopying, recording, or by any information storage and retrieval system, without permission in writing from the publisher.

This book was set in Linotype Helvetica
by Atlantic Typographers
printed on Warren's Cameo Brilliant Dull
by The Meriden Gravure Company
and bound by The Colonial Press, Inc.
in the United States of America

Library of Congress Cataloging in Publication Data

Metz, Don.
  New architecture in New Haven.

1. Architecture — New Haven.
2. Architecture — Designs and plans. I. Title.
NA735.N39M4   1973   720'.9746'8   72-5839
ISBN 0-262-13095-5
     0-262-63045-1 (pbk)

Contents

Introduction
vi

New Haven Common
2

Yale Art Gallery
4

Yale School of Art and Architecture
6

Crawford Manor Housing for the Elderly
8

Laboratory of Clinical Investigation
10

Yale Laboratory of Epidemiology
12

Temple Street Parking Garage
14

Knights of Columbus Headquarters Building
16

New Haven Coliseum
18

Richard C. Lee High School
20

Church Street South Housing
22

Central Services Building
24

SAAB-SCANIA Office and Warehouse Building
26

Standard Paint Store
28

Community Health Care Center
30

Fire Headquarters
32

Wooster Square
34

Towne House on the Park
36

Matthew Ruoppolo Manor Housing for the Elderly
38

Chermayeff Residence
40

Yale University Health Services Building
42

Becton Engineering and Applied Science Center
44

Beinecke Rare Books Library
46

Yale Computer Center
48

David S. Ingalls Rink
50

Greeley Memorial Forestry Laboratory
54

Yale Kline Biology Laboratory
56

Nuclear Structure Laboratory
58

Yale Kline Geology Laboratory
60

Whitney Avenue Fire Station
62

Mitarachi Residence
64

Northern Branch YMCA
66

Ridge Hill School
68

Samuel Morse and Ezra Stiles Residential Colleges
70

Dwight Cooperative Town Houses
74

Mount Zion Seventh-Day Adventist Church
76

West Rock Nature-Recreation Center
78

Oriental Masonic Gardens
80

Gay Residence
82

St. John Vianney Parish Complex
84

Map of New Haven
86

Photo Credits
88

Introduction

The first edition of *New Architecture in New Haven* was published in 1966 at the peak of the city's renewal, redevelopment, and building programs. The late sixties marked the end of a decade of unprecedented architectural activity fostered by energetic political leadership and an enlightened University policy. Vast amounts of federal and state funds made possible the new highways, housing, schools, and industries that shaped the new New Haven. Yale University's building program, led by its new residential colleges and an expanded science campus, produced a record number of new buildings and a master plan for future expansion.

This revised edition of *New Architecture in New Haven* brings the record to date and reflects, in its selection of projects, the change in the nature of architecture as it responds to the social and economic demands of the early 1970's. Federal and state participation in the city's projects, as elsewhere, has dropped off significantly, and the University can no longer afford the risk of the extravagant architectural gesture. The resulting attitude seems to have diminished the quantity but not the quality of architectural expression. Innovative solutions in housing and structural systems have taken priority over the elaborate spatial eloquence of the recent past. Included in this edition is a representative selection of New Haven architecture of the past fifteen years.

New Haven Common

In 1641, John Brockett developed a plan for the City of New Haven based on a symmetrical grid of nine squares. The central square was designated as the Public Common. Surrounding the Common today are various examples of the city's architectural heritage from the last three hundred years. These historic landmarks establish an attitude of scale and variety that is vital to the Common's function as a public park and meeting place in the midst of a busy city. Future projects around the Common must continue to recognize it as a constant point of reference in the changing profile of the city.

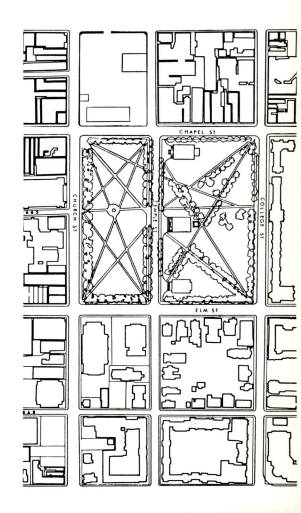

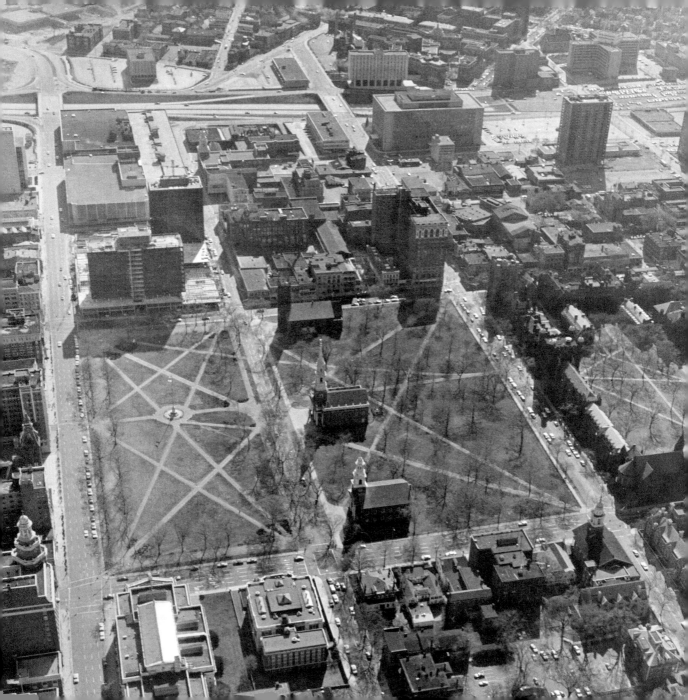

Yale Art Gallery
1111 Chapel Street

architect: Louis I. Kahn

The Yale Art Gallery represents the first important step in the University's architectural renaissance begun in the middle 1950's under the late President Alfred Whitney Griswold. Smooth brick and glass curtain walls sheath four floors of open loft space. The ceilings reveal an innovative, tetrahedron-based structural system that lends a rich texture to the otherwise simplified exhibition areas. Sculpture courts on the north side serve to integrate the museum's interior with the natural privacy of Weir Court.

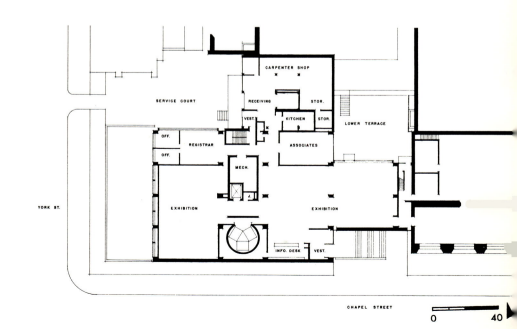

Yale School of Art and Architecture
180 York Street

architect: Paul Rudolph

The Yale School of Art and Architecture is occupied by the graduate departments of painting, city planning, architecture, graphic design, and sculpture. Organized around four massive interior columns, its nine stories are broken into over thirty different levels. A basically open plan allows spaces to compress and explode dramatically as the heights from floor to ceiling change from seven to thirty feet. The rough, ribbed texture of the exterior walls is continued inside, where it is played against orange carpets and smooth partition walls.

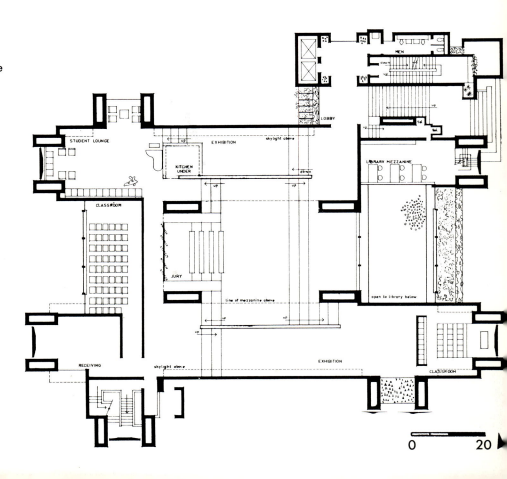

Crawford Manor Housing for the Elderly
North Frontage Road and Park Street

architect: Paul Rudolph

This 15-story residential tower lends quality to the growing quantity of high-rise buildings appearing between the Yale campus and the Oak Street Connector. It is one of the several buildings included in the city's program to provide housing for the elderly. An especially designed, low-cost building-block veneer emphasizes the vertical aspect of the building. A highly fragmented plan and the interactions of the curved protruding balconies combine to produce an active, sculptured façade.

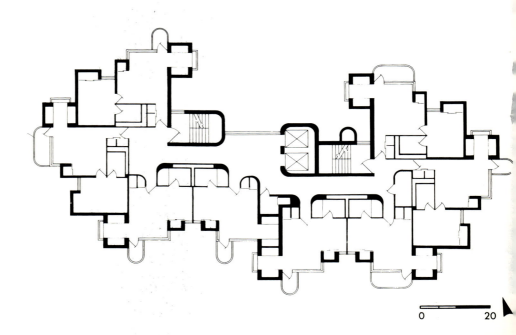

0   20

Laboratory of Clinical Investigation
Howard and Davenport Avenues

architect: Douglas Orr, de Cossy, Winder and Associates

Thoughtful site planning and massing make this laboratory tower a key component of the growing Yale–New Haven Medical building complex. Laboratories and offices are efficiently organized in a pin-wheel plan around the central elevator core. Hung ceilings in the corridors conceal the major mechanical distribution systems servicing each respective floor. Solid oak doors and rough brick walls in the corridors are contrasted with the glass and stainless steel technical apparatus in the adjacent laboratories.

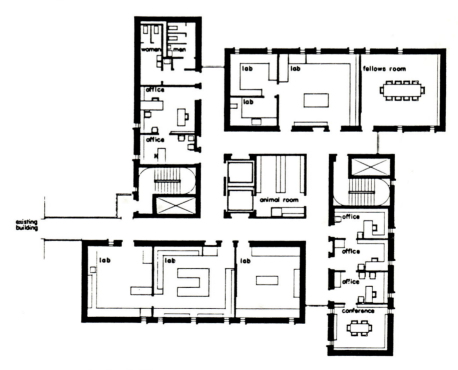

typical floor

Yale Laboratory of Epidemiology
60 College Street

architect: Philip Johnson

Acknowledging the immense scale of the Oak Street Connector and its frontage roads, the Epidemiology Laboratory responds in kind with huge pilasters rising eight stories from an entry-level podium. The building's reinforced-concrete frame is wrapped in a tight symmetrical sandstone and tinted glass veneer. Each floor is individually planned to serve the unique requirements established by respective laboratory needs. Narrow, hooded windows provide a token amount of light to the interior while furnishing a secondary scaling device to the exterior elevations.

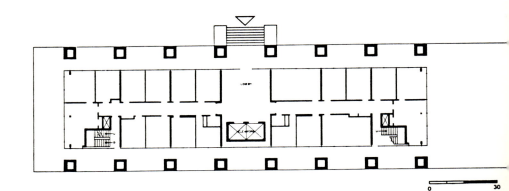

**Temple Street
Parking Garage**
Between Church and Temple
Streets at George Street

architect: Paul Rudolph

Located next to downtown
New Haven's largest department stores, this reinforced-concrete, self-service garage
can accommodate 1,300 cars.
Shoppers park on low-clearance split-level ramps
and walk directly into the
adjacent stores. Stretching the
length of two full city blocks,
the garage is accessible from
cross-city streets and the
Oak Street Connector. The
curved cast-in-place railing
panels, slabs, and columns
are finished in a rugged
form-work texture.

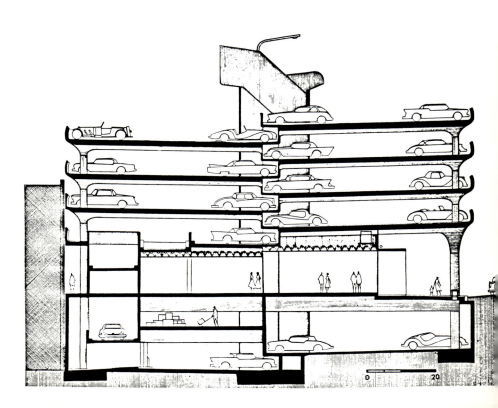

Knights of Columbus Headquarters Building
1 Columbus Plaza

architect: Kevin Roche, John Dinkeloo and Associates

Four cylindrical towers at the corners and a central elevator core provide support for 23 floors of office space in this 320-foot-high building. The tile-clad towers contain stairs, rest rooms, and mechanical equipment. Weathering steel girders and floor structure span 80 feet between towers. The glass curtain wall is held back 5 feet for sun control purposes. The structure is related in scale and materials to the adjacent New Haven Coliseum (designed by the same architect), and the two buildings form an awesome landmark at the major gateway to the city.

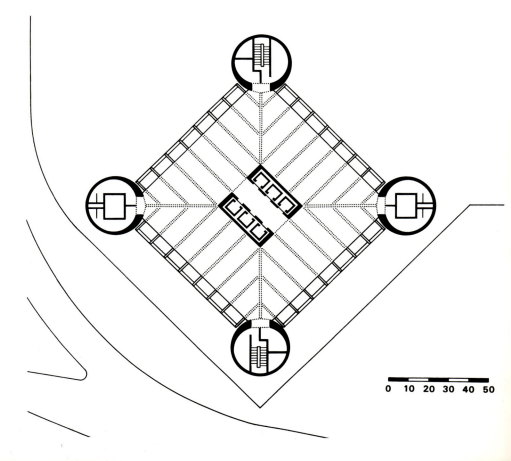

New Haven Coliseum
275 South Orange Street

architect: Kevin Roche, John Dinkeloo and Associates

This immense structure covers 4½ acres on a two-block site and consists of two basic elements: an arena with its related facilities and a 2,400-car, four-level parking garage spanning the arena. The parking garage is reached by two double-spiral ramps located at diagonal corners of the complex. Stairs and elevators move pedestrian traffic to the arena concourse level two stories above the street. Combining the roof of the arena with the structure of the garage allows maximum use of the site without impairing pedestrian access and traffic patterns at street level.

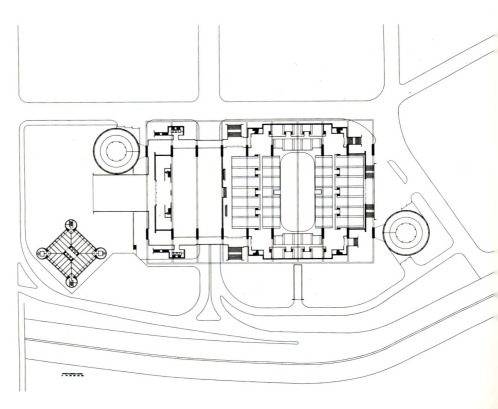

Richard C. Lee High School
100 Church Street South

architect: Kevin Roche, John Dinkeloo and Associates

The high school is based on the house-plan concept. Four houses under one roof are centered around the library. Common facilities, such as special-purpose classrooms, auditorium, and cafeteria, are on the lower level. Physical education facilities are located in the rear and are connected to the main building by a covered passage and bridge. The building is deliberately formal and symmetrical and is meant to suggest both a sense of permanence and the seriousness and dignity of education.

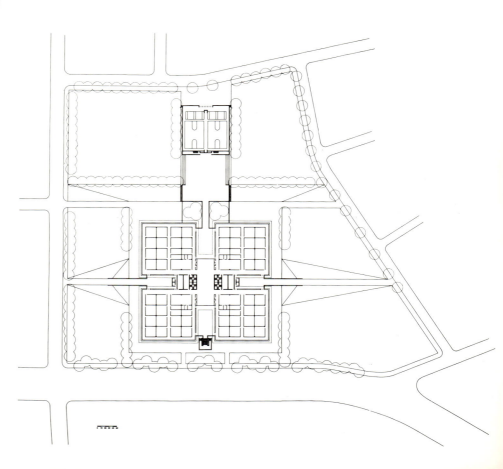

Church Street South Housing
Church Street South

architects: Charles Moore Associates

This controversial housing complex contains 400 units of low-to-moderate-income housing and 309 units of housing for the elderly. Despite a low budget and federal agency red tape, the project has a strong sense of neighborhood vitality. The organizational variety of streets and spaces and the use of bright graphics and street landscaping devices contribute to a cohesive urban environment. Shopping facilities, meeting areas, and community green spaces help define an autonomous community. Perimeter parking and pedestrian walkways allow for the appropriate segregation of people and cars.

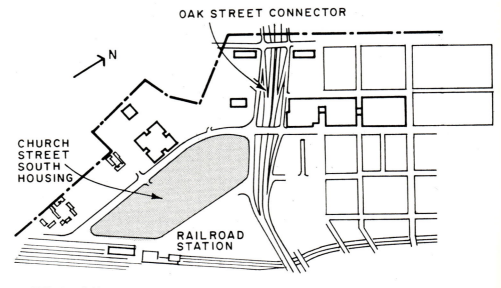

SITE PLAN

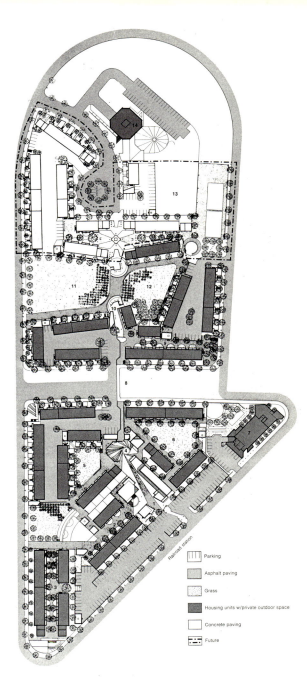

Legend

1	Entrance to pedestrian walk
2	Jose Marti Court
3	Station Court
4	Forum
1-4	Commercial space along walk
5	Christopher Green
6	Cinque Green
7	Robert T. Wolfe Public Elderly Housing
8	Columbus Ave. and location of proposed bridge
9	Malcolm Court
10	Forum
11	Great Green
12	Little Green
13	Housing not built
14	High-rise tower for elderly

Central Services Building
1 State Street

architect: Douglas Orr,
de Cossy, Winder
and Associates

Previously located in separate quarters throughout the city, New Haven's numerous health and welfare agencies are now centralized in this building. Administrative agencies occupy the first-floor offices, which are oriented toward the busy downtown streets. The consulting agencies on the second floor face a large, quiet, interior court. Parking facilities are below the building, along the periphery of the site. Constructed of reinforced concrete throughout, the exterior surfaces are finished in a delicate, vertically ribbed pattern.

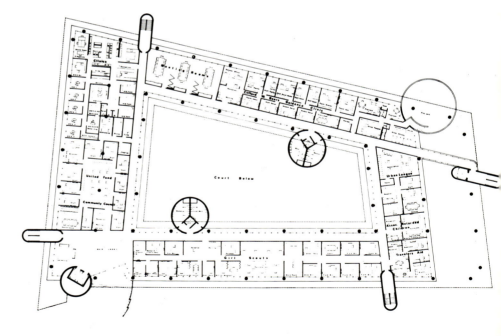

first floor plan

SAAB-SCANIA Office and Warehouse Building
SAAB Drive, Orange

architect: Douglas Orr, de Cossy, Winder and Associates

Sited on a wooden lot adjacent to the Connecticut Turnpike, this 100,000-square-foot building was designed to project a bold visual impact to high-speed traffic while maintaining some sense of human scale when approached by visitors. Typical factory-building components are used efficiently to express the sculptural forms of the west elevation, which serves as both the point of entry and a billboard for the corporate logo.

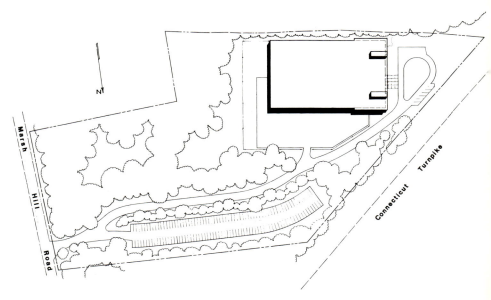

Plot Plan
SCALE: 0' 25' 50'

SAAB

Standard Paint Store
500 Post Road, Orange

architect: James Terrell with
The Environmental Design
Group

Exposed bar joists and mechanical systems, cut-out partitions, and level changes provide an active environment within the walls of this remodeled commercial building located in the midst of a sprawling Route One business strip. The proprietor can maintain visual control from a cashier's cube in the center of the store. Paint and wallpaper displays combined with graphic devices and large geometrical color chips become self-advertising. Incandescent, fluorescent, and natural light sources allow the customer to see a color in its intended atmosphere.

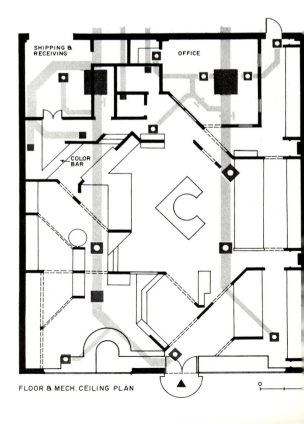

FLOOR & MECH. CEILING PLAN

Community Health Care Center
150 Sargent Drive

architect: Office of Bruce Porter Arneill, A.I.A.

The Community Health Care Center provides comprehensive health care services to 40,000 people annually. The 50,000-square-foot masonry and steel building has the majority of its medical services on the first floor, with administrative and secondary services above. Patients' waiting areas planned around a central courtyard minimize traffic flow to the surrounding consultation and examination rooms. A steel-trussed translucent entrance canopy, judicious use of stairwells, and a variety of window sizes combine to overcome the limitations of the basic rectangular form and a low budget.

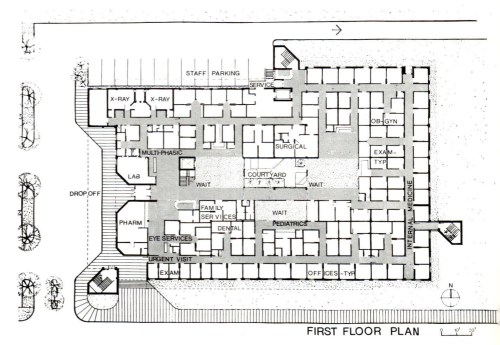

FIRST FLOOR PLAN

Fire Headquarters
952 Grand Avenue

architect: Earl Carlin
design associate: Peter Millard
associate: Paul Pozzi

A compelling structure in its own right, the New Haven Fire Headquarters is especially significant as an effective protest against the traditional dullness of municipal architecture. Four corner towers, responding to the adjacent streets, accentuate the building's angular dynamics. The exterior surfaces are patterned with varying rhythms of vertical grooves. Inside, all structural elements and mechanical apparatus are exposed. The functional integrity of the plan is reinforced by the use of simple and maintenance-free materials throughout the building.

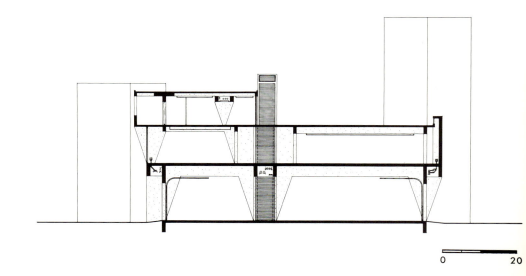

0   20

Wooster Square

The Wooster Square area qualified in 1950 as one of the city's most deteriorated communities. Encouraged by the 1954 housing act, the City Redevelopment office and the ad hoc Wooster Square Renewal Committee established a comprehensive program for rehabilitating the neighborhood. The Conte School, Columbus Mall, Court Street, and Greene Street Housing became the vanguard projects, while hundreds of community-motivated citizens undertook to repair their properties at their own expense. The result is a planned community within the city and the reestablishment of a definitive neighborhood.

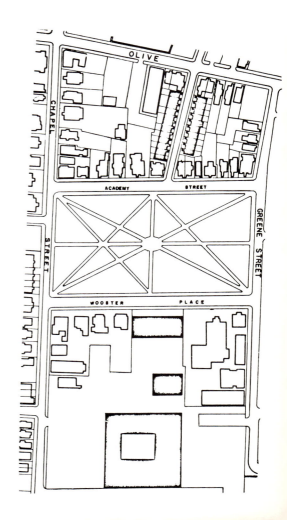

Towne House on the Park
Green Street and Hughes Place

architects: Office of William Mileto

This project contains 36 units of one- and two-bedroom apartments. The one-bedroom units are located a half level below grade, with the two-story, two-bedroom units above. A large enclosed court, removed from street traffic and noise, provides a play area for children. Tenant parking facilities occur to the north of the court. Concrete-block bearing walls and wood joists form the basis of the structural system. Exterior walls, painted an off-white, are punctuated by redwood trim around windows and doors.

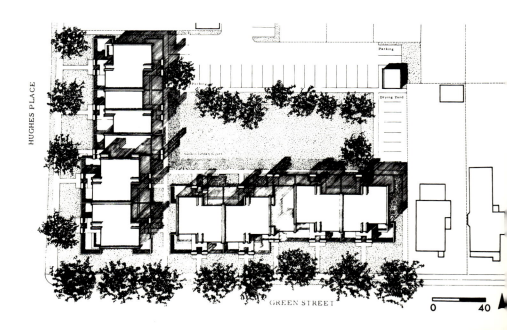

**Matthew Ruoppolo Manor
Housing for the Elderly**
470–480 Ferry Street

architects: Gilbert Switzer and Associates

One of Connecticut's first HUD Turnkey efforts, this 16-unit project makes optimum use of a cramped site while relating inoffensively to its wood-frame, residential neighborhood. Community spaces inside the building open onto the entry court and recreation garden. The Y-shaped plan with a central service core eliminates the need for the long, dreary corridors typical of public housing. Elevator lobbies with large windows are brightly furnished to encourage socializing, and most apartments have private balconies or terraces.

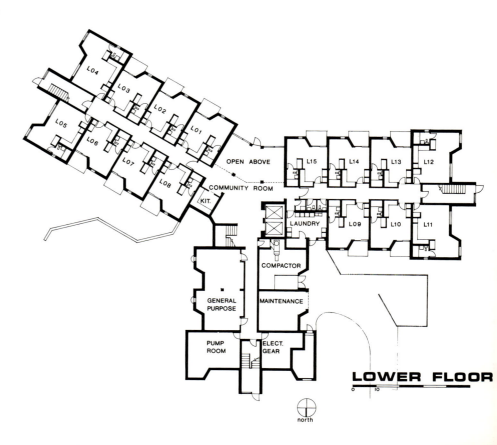

LOWER FLOOR

Chermayeff Residence
28 Lincoln Street

architect: Serge Chermayeff

This one-story house is zoned to provide maximum privacy and quiet. Designed as a variation of the architect's comprehensively developed proposals for medium-density, cluster prototypes, the house performs admirably as an isolated unit on a traditional, residential street. The programmatic needs of three distinct domains with appropriate buffer zones between are logically reflected in the plan. A series of walled courts becomes in fair weather a private extension of interior spaces.

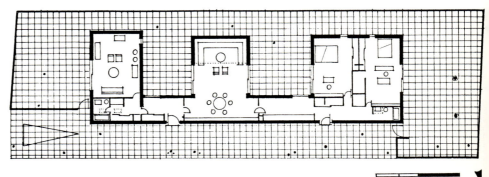

Yale University Health Services Building
17 Hillhouse Avenue

architects: Westermann-Miller Associates

Located at the center of the campus, this six-story limestone and glass building serves the medical needs of the 30,000 people who make up the Yale community. Organized as an affiliate of the Grace-New Haven Hospital, the building provides a wide range of diagnostic and treatment facilities for non-acute health services as a part of a unique prepaid medical health program. A 70-bed infirmary on the fourth and fifth floors can be doubled in case of an epidemic, while a non-appointment clinic for outpatient service is available at entry level.

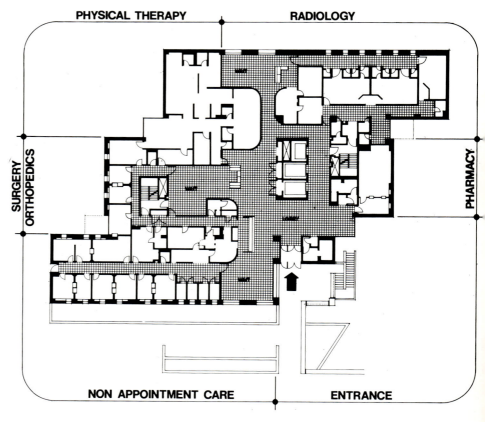

FIRST FLOOR

**Becton Engineering and
Applied Science Center**
3 Hillhouse Avenue

architect: Marcel Breuer

Built only a few feet from the curb, the Becton Laboratory looms massively above Hillhouse Avenue. Six huge concrete columns punctuate an arcade that runs the length of the building at entry level. Uniform grids of precast-concrete panels form the front and rear façades. A departmental library, classrooms, and labs take up the first five floors, with mechanicals on the top floor. Beneath a plaza at the rear of the building is a 275-seat auditorium. Tunnels connect the structure with two adjacent intradepartmental laboratory buildings.

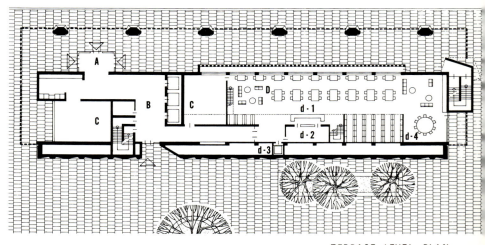

TERRACE LEVEL PLAN

Beinecke Rare Books Library
Wall and High Streets

architect: Gordon Bunshaft of Skidmore, Owings and Merrill

Translucent marble panels admit a warm light to the interior of the boxlike structure that serves as an exhibition area and entry point for this largely subterranean building. Books and manuscripts are stored in a series of climatically controlled stacks. Administrative facilities below ground open to a sunken sculpture court exhibiting a marble landscape by Noguchi. A paved plaza becomes an effective transitional device between this imposing structure and its neoclassic and neo-Gothic neighbors.

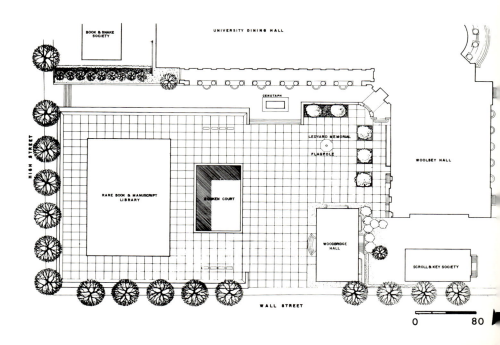

Yale Computer Center
60 Sachem Street

architect: Gordon Bunshaft
of Skidmore, Owings and
Merrill

Located diagonally across Prospect Street from the David S. Ingalls Rink, the Computer Center is a classic example of the Skidmore, Owings and Merrill idiom. Its tinted glass and steel elevations relate inoffensively to the varied architectural heritage of the adjacent buildings. Its precise detailing and machinelike quality are particularly appropriate to the computer technology it serves.

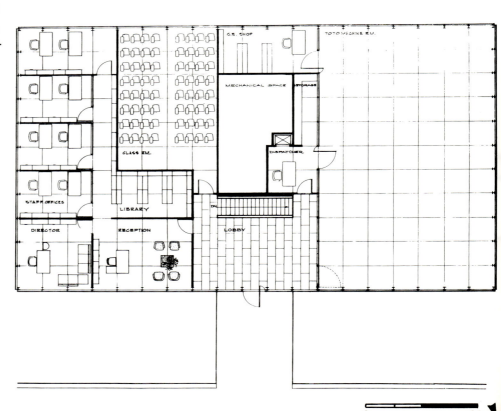

David S. Ingalls Rink
73 Sachem Street

architect: Eero Saarinen

A reinforced-concrete arch spanning 270 feet provides the visual and structural backbone for this controversial skating rink. A system of cables hung between the arch and the low peripheral walls supports a compound-curved wood-plank deck. Exposed mechanical apparatus and the rugged, utilitarian treatment of the interior are skillfully played against the sophisticated contours of the exterior walls and roof.

Greeley Memorial Forestry Laboratory
370 Prospect Street

architect: Paul Rudolph

Solid precast stone walls form a podium beneath the main floor of this multipurpose laboratory. Precast-concrete, Y-shaped columns support a flat roof that overhangs set-back walls. Interior walls stop short of the ceiling, allowing natural light to the interior spaces. A screen suspended from the west end of the roof provides protection from the afternoon sun, as well as providing a means of visually terminating the downhill side of the building.

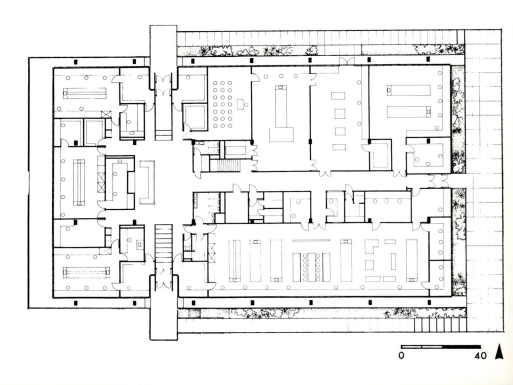

Yale Kline Biology Laboratory
Sachem Street

architect: Philip Johnson

A dramatic addition to the New Haven skyline, the Kline Biology Laboratory forms the hub of the University's burgeoning science-building complex. Dark sandstone and glazed brick form a smooth, muscular skin around the reinforced-concrete frame. Closely spaced, rounded pilasters accentuate the tower's strong vertical aspect. An underground library and twelve stories of laboratories are topped by a floor of dining facilities and a three-story, Parthenon-like mechanical loft.

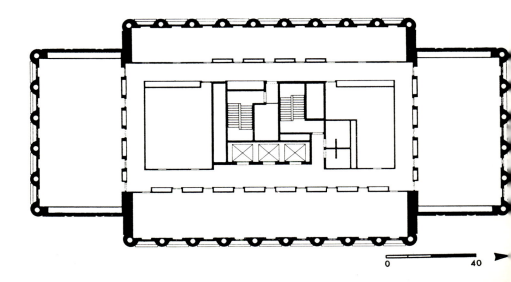

0   40

Nuclear Structure Laboratory
51 Sachem Street

architect: Douglas Orr,
de Cossy, Winder
and Associates

Embedded in the north end of Yale's expanding science complex, the truncated, pyramidic earth forms of the Nuclear Structure Laboratory provide an appropriate sanctuary for the unique Emperor tandem Van de Graaff electrostatic accelerator. The precise, versatile accelerator is 125 feet long, weighs approximately 250 tons, and is capable of generating up to 15 million volts. The huge vault containing the accelerator is adjoined by administrative offices and laboratories for associated research.

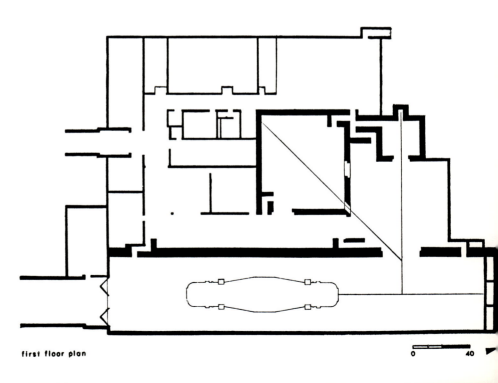

first floor plan

Yale Kline Geology Laboratory
210 Whitney Avenue

architect: Philip Johnson

A spacious, skylit stairway connects three stories of classrooms, laboratories, and offices in this compact, efficiently planned building. Linked by a bridge to the Peabody Museum, the Laboratory is an effective counterbalance to the Museum's neo-Gothic profile. Rounded, protruding vertical forms establish a regular bay system along the glazed brick and dark sandstone façades. Because of the need for consistent, controlled light in the laboratories, fenestration is relatively minimal except for the offices on the north side.

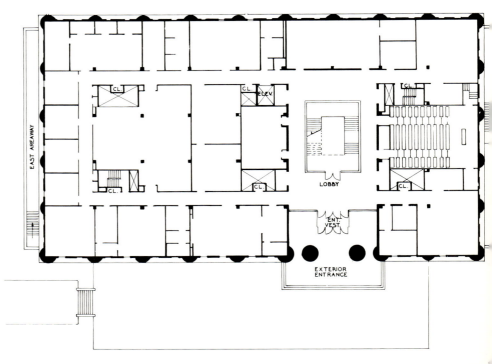

Whitney Avenue Fire Station
352 Whitney Avenue

architect: Earl Carlin
design associate: Peter Millard
associate: Paul Pozzi

Situated on a broad street in a primarily residential area, the Whitney Avenue Fire Station is appropriately scaled to its environment. The dark brick and clapboard-formed concrete exterior is activated by stairways and light wells extending from a basically rectangular plan. Precast T beams span between concrete columns within the sidewalls. The effectively planned firemen's quarters on the second floor reflect a consideration for functional design that is apparent throughout the building.

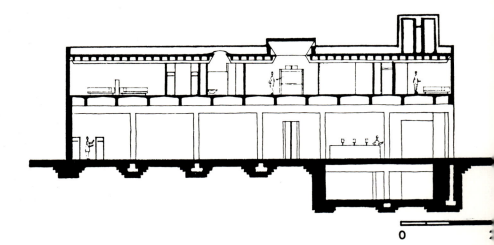

Mitarachi Residence
120 Deepwood Drive, Hamden

architect: Paul Mitarachi

This house was designed to take full advantage of a southern exposure and a dramatic view of New Haven. Because of the sloping site, the house was split into four levels in a basically open plan. All spaces, except for the bedrooms, are oriented southward toward privacy and the view. Circulation space for the entire house is efficiently provided by the stairway and its landings. Laminated wood beams and stud walls are protected for the weather by vertical, tongue-and-groove, Philippine mahogany sheathing.

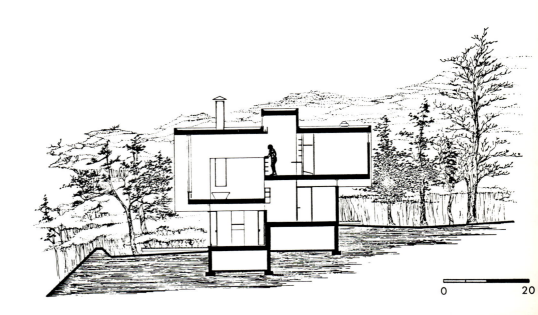

Northern Branch YMCA
1605 Sherman Avenue,
Hamden

architects: Harold Roth –
Edward Saad

Built as the first part of a three-phase program, this structure has a swimming pool and a number of other recreational facilities. A central skylighted hall eases traffic circulation and serves as a common point of entry to the various adjacent facilities. Coffered-concrete floor systems span between brick-bearing walls. Maintenance-free materials throughout, including quarry tile, carpet, and laminated maple, add to the building's attractiveness and durability. Future expansion will include a gymnasium, handball and squash courts, and additional social activity rooms.

Ridge Hill School
120 Carew Road, Hamden

architects: Harold Roth –
Edward Saad

Organized around a team-teaching program using four large learning center areas, the Ridge Hill School enrolls 650 elementary school students in an ungraded curriculum. Efficient interior circulation is achieved via a central sky-lighted rampway connecting the various levels necessitated by a gently sloping site. Vehicular and pedestrian traffic are appropriately segregated, and school bus loading occurs under cover at the lower level. In anticipation of evening and summer use, the plan allows for ready access to community-oriented facilities without disruption of academic areas.

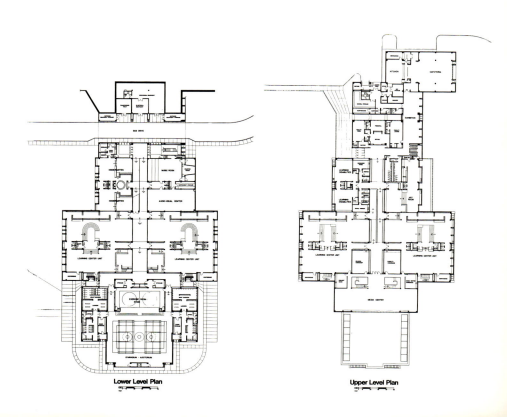

Lower Level Plan   Upper Level Plan

Samuel Morse and Ezra Stiles Residential Colleges
Broadway and Tower Parkway

architect: Eero Saarinen and Associates

The first addition to Yale's residential college system since the 1930's, Morse and Stiles demonstrate a calculated respect for their neo-Gothic neighbors. Gateways, walks, and courtyards establish an effective sequence of spaces between and around the colleges. Ranging in heights from one to thirteen stories, each component of the plan maintains a consistent scale. The carefully integrated sculpture of Constantine Nivola accentuates the project's compelling geometric quality. This quality is continued inside, where polygonal floor plans create a wide variety of residential units.

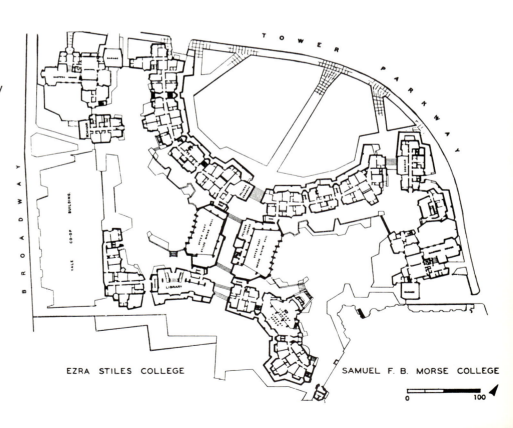

**Dwight Cooperative
Town Houses**
99 Edgewood Avenue

architects: Gilbert Switzer and Associates

The Dwight Coop is an 80-unit town house complex providing a wide range of apartment sizes for low- and moderate-income families. The commendable site plan segregates vehicular and pedestrian traffic and shows potential for versatile development of the interior courtyards. A circular spray pool, playground area, and renovated brick carriage house add to a sense of community, while individual patios and a direct circulation plan allow some degree of privacy.

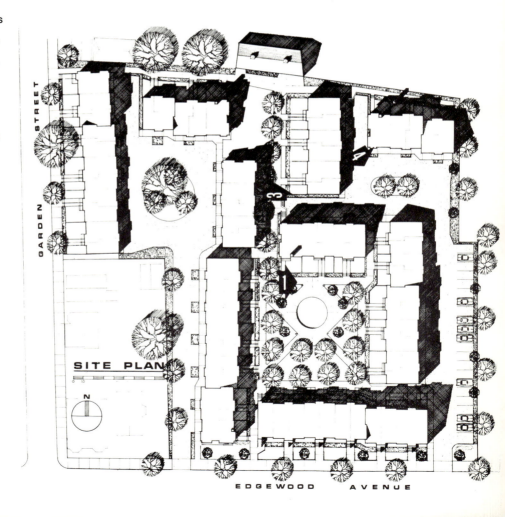

**Mount Zion Seventh-Day
Adventist Church**
64 Marlboro Street, Hamden

architect: Earl Carlin
design associate: Peter Millard
associate: Paul Pozzi

The architectural potential of simple forms and materials is effectively exploited in this low-budget community church. Pews for a congregation of 350 face a chancel that includes the speaker's rostrum, space for a choir of 30, and the baptistry. Custom-made concrete blocks and the fragmentation of exterior volumes significantly reduce the scale of the church to that of its immediate residential environment. The strong, simple quality of each elevation emphasizes the simplicity of the liturgy within.

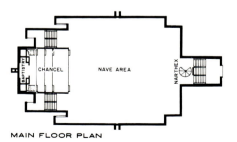

MAIN FLOOR PLAN

LOWER FLOOR PLAN

**West Rock Nature-
Recreation Center**
Wintergreen Avenue

architects: Harold Roth –
Edward Saad

The use of dramatic wood trusses above a system of exposed cedar post, beam, and plank construction gives this small public nature center an informal, rugged appeal.
The building is situated along the entrance walkway to the nature-center grounds near occasional animal shelters. It is used for orientation talks, displays, movies, and related conferences. A staff of three naturalists shares work areas in balcony alcoves above the quarry-tiled exhibit area.

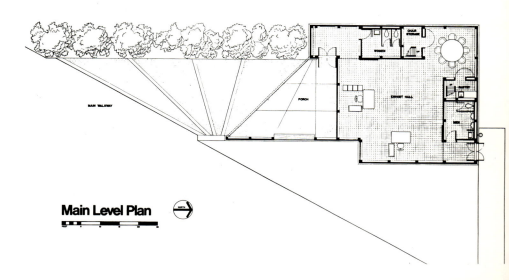

Main Level Plan

Oriental Masonic Gardens
50 Wilmot Road

architect: Paul Rudolph

This low- and moderate-income housing project was assembled with factory-built units stacked together in two-story cruciform configurations. Twelve-foot-wide modules accommodate two- through five-bedroom apartments with living-dining-kitchen areas on the lower floor. The lower and upper floors are at ninety degrees to each other and define two sides of a private courtyard. The plywood modules, with built-in mechanical and structural systems, were assembled in Maryland and trucked to New Haven, where they were craned into place and bolted together.

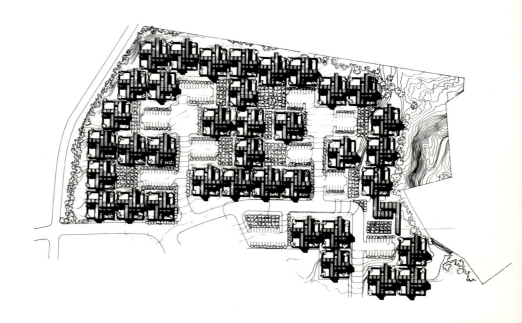

Gay Residence
13 Tulip Tree Lane,
Woodbridge

designer: Don Metz

A central stair system connects four levels of living space, providing varying degrees of privacy in this multizoned home. Inset clerestory glazing, skylights, and window areas make maximum use of the southern exposure and admit direct sunlight most of the day. Built-in furniture, integral with the architecture, occurs throughout the house. Interior finishes include imported tile, red oak floors and woodwork, and white gypsum walls and ceilings. Exterior siding is bleached, quarter-grain fir.

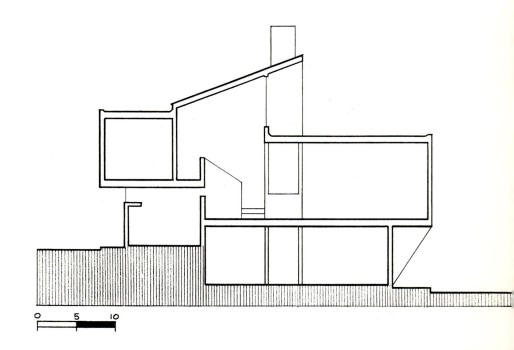

St. John Vianney Parish Complex
Palace and Grove Streets, West Haven

architects: Kosinski Associates

The two interior courts act as buffer zones between church, rectory, and social hall in this parish complex. The three distinct parts are linked by a covered brick arcade, which opens onto a landscaped area adjacent to a parking lot for 200 cars. Philosophical and financial considerations called for a design stressing simplicity and dignity rather than the forms of the traditional monumental temple. In the church wing there is a sparing use of form and materials. Light wells located above the liturgical symbols add to the atmosphere of the religious celebrations.

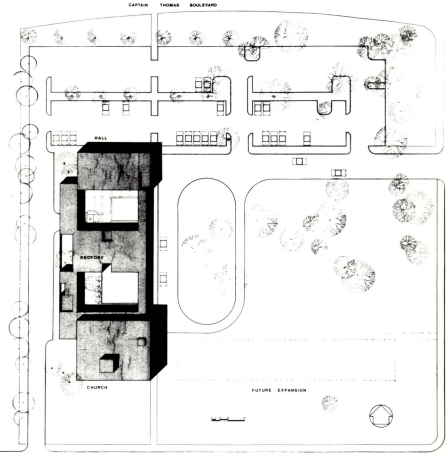

Map of New Haven

2	New Haven Common
4	Yale Art Gallery
6	Yale School of Art and Architecture
8	Crawford Manor Housing for the Elderly
10	Laboratory of Clinical Investigation
12	Yale Laboratory of Epidemiology
14	Temple Street Parking Garage
16	Knights of Columbus Headquarters Building
18	New Haven Coliseum
20	Richard C. Lee High School
22	Church Street South Housing
24	Central Services Building
26	SAAB-SCANIA Office and Warehouse Building
28	Standard Paint Store
30	Community Health Care Center
32	Fire Headquarters
34	Wooster Square
36	Towne House on the Park
38	Matthew Ruoppolo Manor Housing for the Elderly
40	Chermayeff Residence
42	Yale University Health Services Building
44	Becton Engineering and Applied Science Center
46	Beinecke Rare Books Library
48	Yale Computer Center
50	David S. Ingalls Rink
54	Greeley Memorial Forestry Laboratory
56	Yale Kline Biology Laboratory
58	Nuclear Structure Laboratory
60	Yale Kline Geology Laboratory
62	Whitney Avenue Fire Station
64	Mitarachi Residence
66	Northern Branch YMCA
68	Ridge Hill School
70	Samuel Morse and Ezra Stiles Residential Colleges
74	Dwight Cooperative Town Houses
76	Mount Zion Seventh-Day Adventist Church
78	West Rock Nature-Recreation Center
80	Oriental Masonic Gardens
82	Gay Residence
84	St. John Vianney Parish Complex

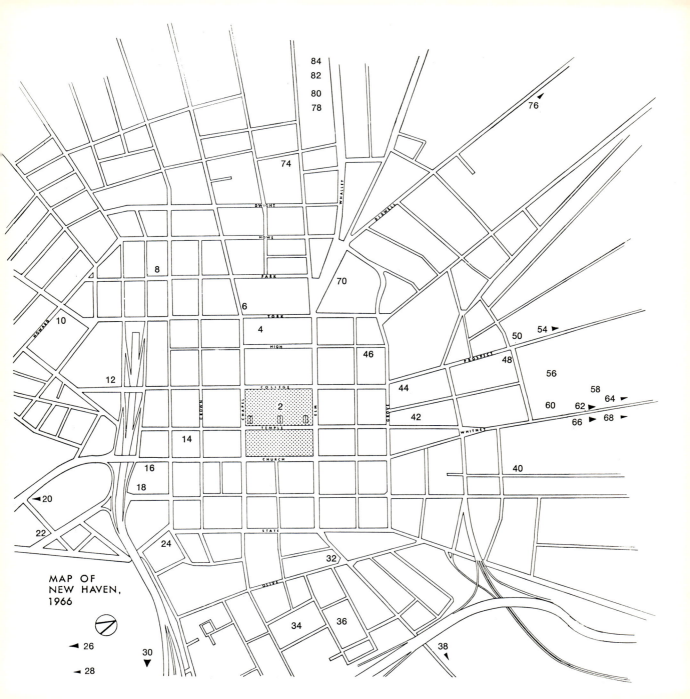

Photo Credits

Introduction	Yuji Noga
New Haven Common	Yuji Noga
Yale Art Gallery	Yuji Noga
Yale School of Art and Architecture	Yuji Noga
Crawford Manor Housing for the Elderly	Yuji Noga
Laboratory of Clinical Investigation	Yuji Noga
Yale Laboratory of Epidemiology	Yuji Noga
Temple Street Parking Garage	Yuji Noga
Knights of Columbus Headquarters Building	Chalmer Alexander
New Haven Coliseum	Chalmer Alexander
Richard C. Lee High School	Ezra Stoller © ESTO
Church Street South Housing	Lee Ryder, A. Wade Perry
Central Services Building	Ezra Stoller © ESTO
SAAB-SCANIA Office and Warehouse Building	Ezra Stoller © ESTO
Standard Paint Store	Robert Perron
Community Health Care Center	Bill Maris
Fire Headquarters	Yuji Noga
Wooster Square	Yuji Noga
Towne House on the Park	Yuji Noga
Matthew Ruoppolo Manor Housing for the Elderly	Thomas A. Brown
Chermayeff Residence	Norman McGrath
Yale University Health Services Building	Bill Rothschild
Becton Engineering and Applied Science Center	Susan Willy
Beinecke Rare Books Library	Yuji Noga
Yale Computer Center	Yuji Noga
David S. Ingalls Rink	Yuji Noga
Greeley Memorial Forestry Laboratory	Yuji Noga
Yale Kline Biology Laboratory	Yuji Noga
Nuclear Structure Laboratory	Yuji Noga
Yale Kline Geology Laboratory	Yuji Noga
Whitney Avenue Fire Station	Yuji Noga
Mitarachi Residence	Yuji Noga
Northern Branch YMCA	Robert Perron
Ridge Hill School	Robert Perron
Samuel Morse and Ezra Stiles Residential Colleges	Yuji Noga
Dwight Cooperative Town Houses	Thomas A. Brown
Mount Zion Seventh-Day Adventist Church	Yuji Noga
West Rock Nature-Recreation Center	Robert Perron
Oriental Masonic Gardens	Donald Luckenbill
Gay Residence	Susan Willy
St. John Vianney Parish Complex	McLeod